HORRID HURRICANES

by Noah Leatherland

Minneapolis, Minnesota

Credits
Images are courtesy of Shutterstock.com. With thanks to Getty Images, Thinkstock Photo, and iStockphoto. Cover – Best-Backgrounds. Recurring – hugolacasse, donatas1205. 2–3 – ComicSans. 4–5 – NDStock, Florian Nimsdorf. 6–7 – Zenobillis, Ryan DeBerardinis. 8–9 – Victoria Sergeeva, Titus JP. 10–11 – Artsiom P. 12–13 – Paul Dempsey, Bilanol. 14–15 – Frame Stock Footage. 16–17 – Alex Erwin, Staff Sgt. Randy Redman of the US Air Force, Public domain, via Wikimedia Commons. 18–19 – Triff, Memories Over Mocha. 20–21 – Alan Budman, Cire notrevo. 22–23 – Trong Nguyen, Frame Stock Footage.

Bearport Publishing Company Product Development Team
Publisher: Jen Jenson; Director of Product Development: Spencer Brinker; Editorial Director: Allison Juda; Editor: Cole Nelson; Editor: Tiana Tran; Production Editor: Naomi Reich; Art Director: Kim Jones; Designer: Kayla Eggert; Designer: Steve Scheluchin; Production Specialist: Owen Hamlin

Library of Congress Cataloging-in-Publication Data is available at www.loc.gov or upon request from the publisher.

ISBN: 979-8-89577-079-5 (hardcover)
ISBN: 979-8-89577-526-4 (paperback)
ISBN: 979-8-89577-196-9 (ebook)

© 2026 BookLife Publishing
This edition is published by arrangement with BookLife Publishing.

North American adaptations © 2026 Bearport Publishing Company. All rights reserved. No part of this publication may be reproduced in whole or in part, stored in any retrieval system, or transmitted in any form or by any means, electronic, mechanical, photocopying, recording, or otherwise, without written permission from the publisher. Bearport Publishing is a division of FlutterBee Education Group.

For more information, write to Bearport Publishing, 3500 American Blvd W, Suite 150, Bloomington, MN 55431.

CONTENTS

Our Home 4

Hurricanes 6

Name That Danger! 8

Hurricane Parts 10

Different Damages 12

Studying Storms 14

Hurricane Hunters 16

Daring Data 18

Staying Safe 20

Safe Studies 22

Glossary 24

Index 24

OUR HOME

Check out our home planet, Earth! It has everything we need to live. However, not everything on Earth is very nice . . .

Earth can sometimes be a dangerous place. Some things on our planet can **damage** land and buildings. Others can cause death!

A volcano

LET'S LEARN ABOUT HORRID HURRICANES!

HURRICANES

What are hurricanes? They are very large storms that blow in circles. Hurricanes can bring heavy rain and strong winds.

A hurricane seen from space

Hurricanes form over warm ocean water. Sometimes, they move toward land. This makes the storms dangerous for people who live nearby.

NAME THAT DANGER!

These storms are called different things depending on where they start. When they form near North America and the Caribbean, they are called hurricanes.

These storms in the Indian Ocean are named cyclones. Typhoons start near East Asia.

HURRICANE PARTS

Eye

The middle of a hurricane is called the eye. It is very calm inside.

Next to the eye is the eye wall. This is where the stormy winds and rain are the strongest.

Eye wall

DIFFERENT DAMAGES

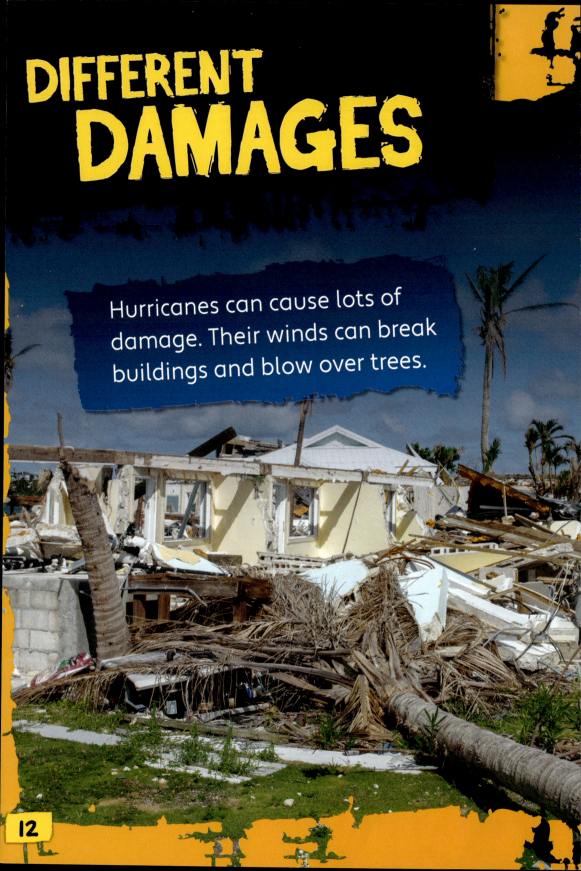

Hurricanes can cause lots of damage. Their winds can break buildings and blow over trees.

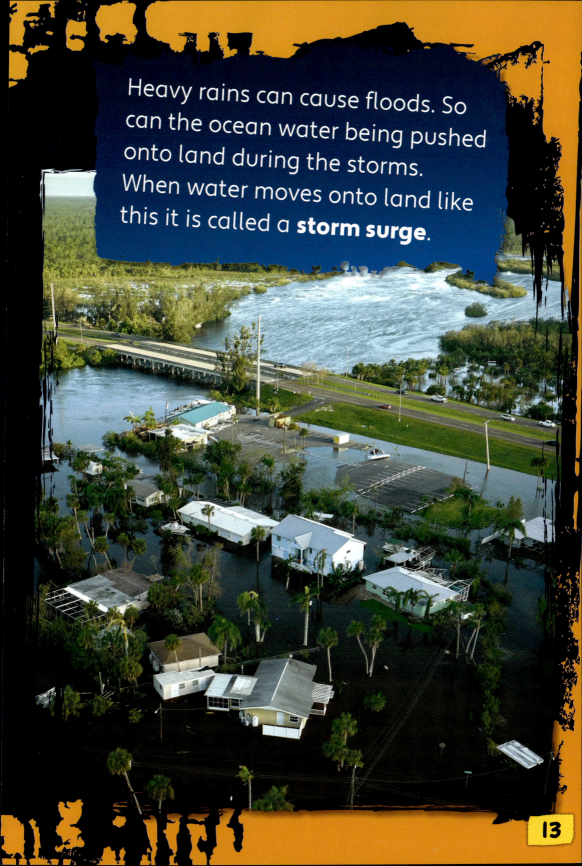

Heavy rains can cause floods. So can the ocean water being pushed onto land during the storms. When water moves onto land like this it is called a **storm surge**.

STUDYING STORMS

Meteorologists (mee-tee-uh-RAH-luh-jists) are scientists who study the weather. They use information about what's happening in the **atmosphere** to **predict** the weather.

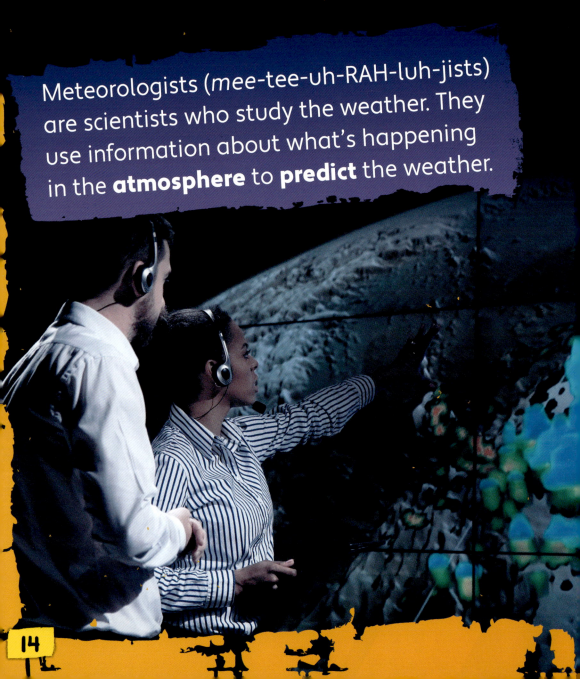

The atmosphere tells meteorologists if it will be hot or cold. It also helps them spot where a hurricane might form.

HURRICANE HUNTERS

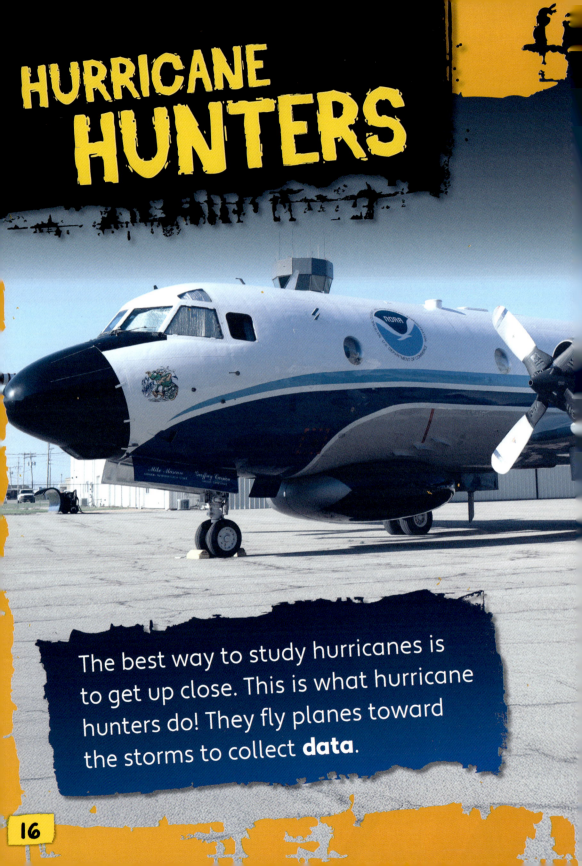

The best way to study hurricanes is to get up close. This is what hurricane hunters do! They fly planes toward the storms to collect **data**.

The planes drop machines called dropsondes. As they fall, dropsondes collect data. The data is then sent to meteorologists.

A dropsonde

DARING DATA

Meteorologists use the collected data to predict things about the storm. They try to figure out how a hurricane will move.

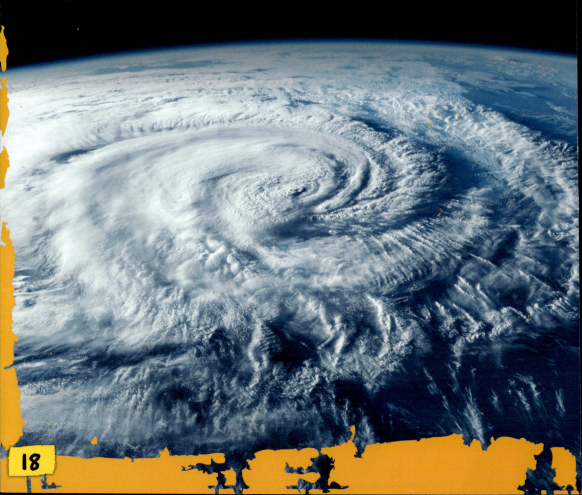

If a hurricane is coming, meteorologists send out warnings. These messages help people prepare to keep themselves safe.

STAYING SAFE

HURRICANE COMING

EVACUATE NOW!

What should you do during a hurricane warning? Go to the nearest **shelter**.

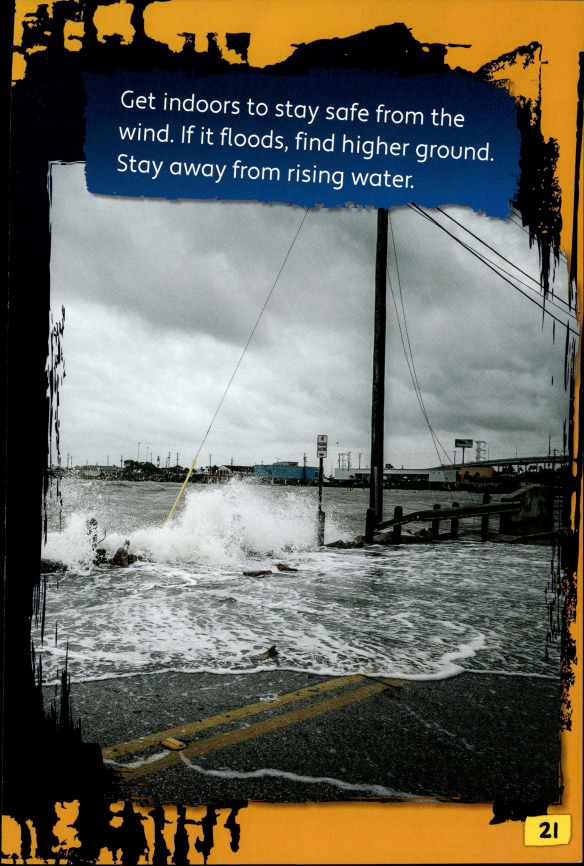
Get indoors to stay safe from the wind. If it floods, find higher ground. Stay away from rising water.

SAFE STUDIES

Hurricanes are super interesting to learn about. However, they can be very dangerous.

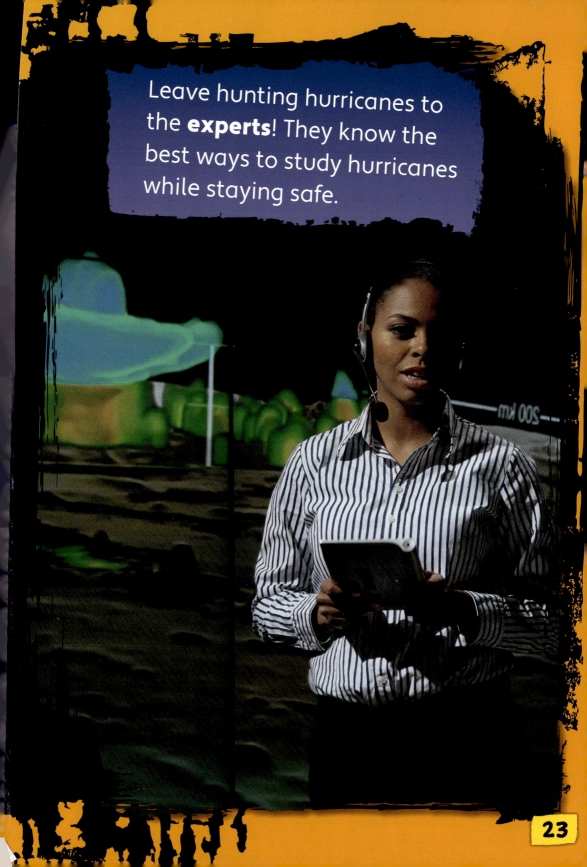

Leave hunting hurricanes to the **experts**! They know the best ways to study hurricanes while staying safe.

GLOSSARY

atmosphere the mixture of gases that surrounds Earth

damage harm

data information

experts people who know a lot about a subject

predict to make a guess based on facts

shelter a place where you can stay safe

storm surge the rise of water due to storms or hurricanes

INDEX

data 16–18
land 5, 7, 13
meteorologists 14–15, 17–19
planes 16–17

rain 6, 11, 13
shelters 20
storms 6–9, 13, 16, 18
water 7, 13, 21
wind 6, 11–12, 21